MEDICINE YEAR

Poems by Thomas R. Smith

Published in 2022 by Paris Morning Publications
parismorningpublications.com

Copyright ©Paris Morning Publications
All rights reserved. No part of this book may be used or reproduced
without written permission from the publisher except in the case of brief
quotations embodied in critical articles and reviews.

Published and printed in the United States of America
ISBN: 978-0-578-37981-4

Cover illustration by John Ilg
Cover design by Audrey Campbell

CONTENTS

For the healers,
and for Krista
"Your good heart. Your awake, alive mind."

INTRODUCTION:

HEALING SONGS

Medicine Year is a record in poems of 2020, a year in which, for my wife Krista and me, personal crises coincided with the coronavirus pandemic in a medical "perfect storm," a triple whammy the likes of which we'd never experienced.

Here's the story: On December 23, 2019, a little less than four months before the lockdowns began in earnest, I was tentatively — and, it turned out, correctly — diagnosed with prostate cancer. That evening, emotionally shocked, I began to nod out over supper and Krista insisted on hurrying me to the ER. By then I'd mostly pulled out of my swoon. It was late, and I was only half-cognizant of how drained Krista looked. The doctor on duty asked if she was OK, and should they check her? She told him she was all right, just tired. When we returned home after midnight, Krista collapsed asleep on our bed still in her day clothes. I covered her with a blanket, nestled into her, and uneasily surrendered to my exhaustion.

In the morning, Christmas Eve day, I couldn't rouse her to normal wakefulness. Her listlessness and lethargy made clear that something was wrong. Struggling her into coat and boots, an awkwardly new catheter night-bag hooked to my belt under my long winter coat, I drove us back to the ER where after hours of waiting and testing on the busy holiday it was determined that Krista had suffered a hemorrhagic stroke in her right frontal brain lobe. She was rushed by ambulance to United Hospital in St. Paul, 30 miles away, where we then spent our Christmas or what would have been our Christmas. Deeply worrisome days followed with each in our own medical limbo.

After a disheartening false start, Krista began to make progress in rehab at Courage Kenny Rehabilitation Institute at United in the new year. As for myself, I eventually had surgery to stabilize my condition. After three months away, Krista returned home, by which time the pandemic had ratcheted up to full strength. For us, most of 2020 was essentially a matter of recovering together from our individual ills while trying to dodge the new threat of COVID. The poems in this book chart that year that tested us and changed our lives.

Early on I found it easier to write about Krista's ordeal than my own. I had become a warrior on her behalf, protective in a way I'd never before experienced in our marriage of more than 35 years. It was only later, when I saw Krista out of immediate danger, that I could concentrate on myself. Of course I was at least half-crazy most of this time, maybe still am. Being by nature not a "confessional" poet, I've kept my privacy about my own medical travails, except where these poems' narrative demanded otherwise. Certainly the hardest thing for me that year was not being able to share with Krista, my life partner and soul mate, what I was experiencing.

These events constitute the background of all the poems in *Medicine Year*, and occasionally the foreground too. There are several kinds of poems here from love poems to topical poems to spiritual poems to poems of natural observation, these last a sustainable source of nourishment in times that deplete our physical and emotional resources.

I want the reader to understand that this book is fundamentally *not* about illness or pandemic but about *health and being alive* during a year in which I truly began to see how precious life is. These poems are healing songs I wrote primarily to keep myself afloat emotionally.

A word about how this book is structured: A rule I set for *Medicine Year* is that the poems' order must be strictly chronological. The contents are limited to the year 2020 with a couple of exceptions: since our disasters began with the last week of 2019, I've balanced the two poems from that week with a pair from the first week of 2021, making the time period covered here a total of 54 weeks. A dream on New Year's morning, 2021, gifted me with a hopeful vision of post-pandemic life for the book's penultimate entry. The poems are individually dated, making this book as close to a poetic diary as I'll likely come to publishing. Ever since learning of *The Year of My Life* by the classical Japanese haiku poet Issa, I've entertained the idea of doing such a collection myself, and 2020 was my year for it if ever there was one.

The reader may notice in the progression of these poems a kind of inverted emotional bell curve reflecting the available daylight from season to season. The darker poems tend to belong to the winter months, with an easing in spring and summer, shadows gathering again as we approach what I call in one poem "our dreaded anniversaries." This inverted curve seems to give the book a beginning, a middle, and if not an end, then a continuation, a new cycle begun. As Eliot said, "In my end is my beginning."

Writing in early 2022, I acknowledge that our COVID ills may be far from over. The hopeful dream of my New Year's poem remains just that for the moment, a dream. I might have extended this chronicle farther forward into the present, but I like the wintery parenthesis around the 2020 poems, so there they will stand. There's no year that is not, for someone, somewhere, a "medicine" year, in need of whatever healing songs come to hand. Whatever comes, I hope the reader also will find some healing in following our medicine year.

Prologue: 2019

MISSISSIPPI JOHN AGAIN

Returning downhearted to the hospital
parking ramp, I start the car, and
the CD I was playing earlier,
Mississippi John Hurt's *Today!*, comes on
again — *Make me a pallet down soft and
low, make me a pallet on your floor.*

What was it about John that was so
nourishing, even healing to us
alienated white kids in the Sixties?
In a moment of frightening, turbo-
charged change bearing down on us and our world,
his voice offered what we longed for
but which the adult life we were growing into
withheld — an earthy warmth, a human
eros, a dignity, a kindness.

I suppose that's why I still pull John Hurt
off the shelf when I'm feeling empty and
forlorn, as I do after this hospital
visit. Now I'm feeding the ticket and bills
into the pay station lit and tinseled
for Christmas. There happens to be an actual
person in the booth, and exiting I turn
to wave. An older Black man waves back,
his round face and heavy-lidded eyes looking
uncannily like those of Mississippi John.
I know I must take this as an omen.

December 28

"YOU DON'T KNOW WHAT LOVE IS"

Rehab, New Year's Eve

You can only watch, encourage as she
slowly lifts each forkful of mashed
potatoes, chicken, and carrots to her mouth.
She is deliberate, slow in her wheel-
chair perched higher than you. Tired and
undemonstrative after the rigors of
the day's therapy, she speaks only
with her eyes. Those eyes send you back
to all that wishful talk in your teens and
twenties about "love," to which you pretended
knowledge. *Kid, you want to know what love
looks like?* the present moment asks that far-
back would-be Romeo. Don't take your eyes
off the woman in the wheelchair lifting
with such care and effort her mashed potatoes.

December 31

2020

2020

JANUARY

Let me be well with the silence

LAUGH AT ME

Here I am brushing my teeth in my
plaid nightshirt and that funny, loose
little felt cap you made and gave to me,
looking like some comic peasant out of
Bruegel, and the only thing missing
to complete the moment is you sharing
a laugh at the gentle humor of it.

January 4

PRAYER

I need patience to hope, so give me patience.
Let me trust as I did once in Time the Healer.
Let me rest in the assurance of things greater
than the seen, the cupped hand holding us all.
Let me be easy with the moment and not stand
in its way like a tree fallen across a stream.
Don't let despair eclipse my faithfulness.
Let me not resist the winter, remembering
that every winter is followed by a spring.
Let the green root rest and take strength
in the winter earth until the sun lifts it.
Meanwhile let me be well with the silence.
Let me be brave as I was when I
had nothing to lose but myself.

January 5

AN AIDE NAMED HAILE

1.

All afternoon, New Year's Day, she lay
silent. As the clock hands turned toward darkness
I put on my coat to go. A downturn
from yesterday's eating and occasional
speaking. The nurses gazed into their screens.
I felt the loneliness grow around me.

2.

I had read his name on the room chart.
"Is that *Haile*?" I asked. "My full name is
Haile Selassie, but I go by Haile."
"You must be from Ethiopia," I said.
He liked that I got that. "My parents named
me, but I don't want to be Emperor!"

3.

Now here he stood, with his arms thrown wide,
the one person on the unit who'd moved toward
my grief and pain. "Happy New Year," he said
gently. "Oh I hope so!" And Haile
Selassie hugged me, called me "Brother."
Beautiful human gift in a strange land.

January 6

KRISTA'S FEET

You will put on shoes again.
You will bend to tie the laces.
You will stand once more of your own
volition on those self-shod feet.
Everything that feet do your feet will do again.
You will walk beside our beloved Kinnickinnic
in the morning. In winter, your feet will test
cautiously the ice. Swelling will go down,
weakness subside, muscle tone return.
The light seed inside each sole
that is the spark of dance will grow again
with the springtime. You will step lightly,
light-heartedly to music. Earth will again play
the happy red carpet to your star-stride.

January 7

THE SADNESS

Three weeks out the sadness hits her —
the injured brain struggles to understand,
but hasn't yet the strength to wrap around
what has actually happened. When asked by
the psychologist, a kind man, how she feels,
she replies, "Wild detour" or "I'm working
on a detective case." There's a knowing
wit behind the way she phrases it, but
underneath she's dead serious — there's really
nothing to laugh at in these misaimed throws
of sentences. And when in her exhaustion
the sorrow seeps up from below to claim
her face, I long for the day when she can
tell me how it was with her — words held
hostage by confusion, assurances
of those busying around her thin
indeed — as her tears waited on time's
healing to find their old channels. And
I don't want her to see how sad I am,
though how can she not read it in my eyes?

January 14

LOOKING UP AND LOOKING DOWN

Another sunset we can't see behind the January gray. Yet some hints of cream, clouds brightening a little. A woman approaches, being led by a black dog. She's glancing up at something, smiling — a bald eagle circles the river, in great luxurious orbits. The woman and I exchange greetings. Passing her, I look down to see on the dark water below the bridge trumpeter swans. I count ten, so close I can clearly discern the delicate shadings of warm gray on the juveniles' backs, which often look dingy from a distance and will someday give way to the whiter-than-white of adult plumage, as these overcast winter days will give themselves over to bright springtime. Now they float together, sumptuous as centerpieces on tables of the rich. Look up, look down. We are all those rich. This is our table.

January 28

CLIMBING THE STAIRS

The PT team, Jen and April, want
Krista to try climbing some stairs. We're out
on the eighth-floor landing, looking up
a flight of ten steps. Krista has been
practicing walking in the hallway,
but this takes it to a whole new level.
She starts shaky but, one woman below her
and the other above, she's staying upright,
arms stretched wide to grip handrails on both
sides. Her hesitations make clear what hard
work this is. The top of the flight seems
high up indeed, even precarious.
I can see her fresh sense of shock in
having lost the ability to do this
easily, and the scary accomplishment
of standing in her weakened state on
that summit. Slowly she arrives there
under her own power, by her own effort.
But the achievement will not be complete
until she turns and steps down again,
slowly, her face registering the full
mix of fear, exhilaration, and
disbelief. *Balance weight on handrails,
left foot down, then right.* And she has reached
the eighth-floor landing where she started.
Later she tells me, "It makes me want to
cry," and does. "That felt profound. And I'm
glad you were there to share it with me."

January 28

FEBRUARY

Bare trees are shaking in the wind

44 DAYS

1.

After forty-two of Krista's forty-four
days at United, a nursing assistant
named Dave tells me, "Sometimes the next day
a person is gone and we're the last ones
to have performed some kind act for them.
I've worked here seven years, and that's happened
to me a few times. It feels important."
Dave smiles. "The best thing is when we see
someone leave recovered and strong again."

2.

When Krista had been a week in hospital
for her stroke, attempts were being made,
unsuccessfully, to get her walking.
A nurse named Tara told how she'd observed
my wife leaning to one side on the bed
and drooling, and told the doctors, "This woman
isn't ready." Thus her advocacy
kept Krista in Intensive Care at
a critical moment. Gratitude to Tara!

3.

During Krista's six weeks at United,
I have practically lived there myself,
witnessed the stops and starts, the gains
and setbacks, and overarching it all,
every day, a dedication to caring
that humbles me. No one would choose to be
in the hospital, yet I'm certain

there are few places on this earth where
one can get as close to heaven.

February 2

LIVING ALONE AGAIN FOR A WHILE

The first week was crushingly lonely,
especially the nights. Her absence shouted
from every surface, every little thing
she'd had a hand in, which over forty
years was almost everything. Gradually
you got used to it, even, in certain
moods and moments, relished it: you hadn't
been on such good terms with yourself since
you were that freewheeling bachelor, the self
that had attracted her in the first place.
At some point we must take responsibility
for our lives: you know that, in the abstract.
But it's another matter when you find yourself
actually doing it, washing the dishes,
half-listening to public radio,
only occasionally now noticing
the strangeness of this home you did not
make alone but with her collaboration
on every detail — a true work of art —
and how different it is from where you
thought you lived the day before the stroke.

February 9

WEATHER REPORT

Out west a blizzard is sweeping into the state,
bitter cold following close behind. We're at the edge,
won't receive the full brunt, though you wouldn't know
it from the way the bare trees are shaking in the wind.
Thin snow hurries across the yards, as if trying
to weave some picture that keeps unraveling
before it can be resolved by the viewer's eye.

We've survived many storms before this one, chances are
we'll be OK. But I worry about the people in
the Care Center — a woman died yesterday,
a man today. Winters are hardest on the weak.
How strong is anyone? We must do what we can.
Write a check to the relief organization.
Dump a bag of seed on the ground so birds can eat.

February 12

VALENTINE'S DAY AT THE CARE CENTER

We're the youngest couple at the Sweetheart Luncheon.
Collectively, we and the other six couples have been
married for over 400 years. But how few in the facility
have spouses to eat with. We couples are far outnumbered
by those having their regular lunch in the dining hall.
For this noon hour the chapel has been transformed to a
temporary cafe, albeit a Jesus-themed one. There's that
old painting of the Lord sitting in an idyllic garden with
perfectly dressed and groomed 1950's kids around him:
Suffer the Little Children. White tablecloths, cheerful
young servers, champagne (although Al at our table has to
have his thickened). Some favorite farm stories are being
told in this room. Two old husbands remember, as boys,
being repulsed by the spectacle of chicken butchering. "I
didn't want to see the body running around without the
head." "Me either!" How strange it is to simply wake to
the moment. We have never seen a Valentine's Day like
this one. It would be ungracious to complain. Clearly
we're exactly where we need to be.

February 14

TUCKING IN

One night before I left to go home,
you asked me to tuck you in.
Now, you say, at bedtimes
you think of that simple, comforting
gesture. And now I imagine
you tucking me into our half-empty
bed! I've missed you in so many
ways, alone in the house for
almost two months. Meanwhile your
brain grows daily around matters
it must grasp. I also am chewing
a hard loaf. No need
to worry. You are returning.
I watch you grow toward
the light like the springtime.

February 15

ORDINARY LIFE

Was it Emerson who wrote that marriage
is an improvement on love? Today, taking
your arm and helping you from the car into
Noodles & Company after your follow-
up appointment with the cardiologist,
I can't tell the difference. In a sunny
booth I tell you how fine it is to simply
see you across a restaurant table
again, our first such outing in two months,
fresh again as if for the first time.
Thousands of meals I took for granted,
my mind absent, not seeing or hearing you.
Maybe nothing will ever be
ordinary like that for us again —
and maybe that's a good thing — except
what we choose to honor by pretending
it so, while knowing the fragile value
of our happiness and how in an instant
it can turn into something else.

February 27

LEAP DAY

Bonus day wedged between February and March. Persistent cold and lengthening light mixing messages. Body and spirit pine for spring, but winter withholds. Yet there are signs: snow gradually shrinks away from the foot of a tree. The exposed earth looks disheveled, stiff, unready, but the geese are all over her, already scouting riverfront locations for nest-building. The horns of the crescent moon will ride the night sky, fatten to full, starve, fatten toward Easter. Those impatient with spring get sick, lose a few days to sleep. How beautiful in the morning the hoar-frosted cedar needles!

February 29

MARCH

Make me the springtime

THE GIFT DESPITE

Today, the Care Center on lockdown for
the coronavirus, we visited
a few minutes through the window of your room,
touched fingertips against the screen. I refilled
the feeder so the sparrows watching
from the arborvitae would come flocking
to the board to keep you company.
All that time I kept half an eye on your
face, shadowy behind the glass as one
of those veiled women in purdah.
Disaster throws obstacles between us
and the future we thought probable
just weeks ago. Meanwhile there's the present
distance and separation, gratuitous
hardship. We must call on our durable
connection, remember everything
we've been to each other, that richness
to which we add the gift of this moment.

March 13

THE LONELINESS

Already a vast loneliness has seeped
into our souls with the cancellations
and closings. We miss the conviviality
of the restaurant table, the church service,
the joy of the jamming musicians,
the natural camaraderie of
sidewalk and supermarket. We're not
meant to be alone, not meant to deflect
the approach of neighbors. Now each locked-down
house becomes a grave where small, dismembered
pieces of community lie scattered alive,
waiting to be called back to wholeness.
We ache for each other, ache for contact.
We knew it would all break down someday.
Not sustainable. *The center cannot hold.*
We are being shown something bigger.
We are being called to something higher.

Shall we come out of this changed, finally
able to hear each others' voices across
the social distance, the voices drowned out
by fear? When the theaters and bars reopen,
when the hospital beds are vacant again
and the world resumes its old business
of getting and spending, how shall we think
on these days withdrawn from one another
and the communal heart, the dead civic air?
Will the grief still eat at us, as it does now?
Is this how it happens, a lesson we need
to learn, overshadowing all our other

learning? In the enforced quiet we have
space to ask these questions and listen
for answers. How will we love each other
and ourselves in the upheavals to come?

March 19

"YOU'LL NEVER WALK ALONE"

I think it scared me a little, as a kid —
the emotionality, the near-religious gravity.
I mostly heard "storm" and "be afraid."
I sensed that it was about something big.
Now it's come round again,
in a 1963 version by Gerry and the Pacemakers
that probably didn't get much play on our shores
so it sounds old yet fresh to my ears.

That recording was enlisted by the Dutch DJ
Sander Hoogendoorn to comfort Europeans
fearful and house bound as we are here in the States,
broadcast simultaneously on March 20th
on hundreds of radio stations from Finland
to Romania, Luxembourg to Spain.
There's a video of the old song that fits
perfectly this moment of the pandemic,

the most uplifting I've seen in weeks.
In the video dozens of different
people mime Gerry Marsden's vocal,
men and women, adults and children, some funny
but all of them sweet and profoundly moving
as they throw themselves into their part of the lyric,
letting some essential innocence and vulnerability,
which we all feel so keenly now, shine through.

My body gets sad having to hold itself
at a distance from so many I love. Doesn't yours?
These stand-ins, with their serious working class
faces, throw their arms around each other, sway together

as they sing in that old familiar warm way
we've suddenly lost. The lonely have
always known that touch is the true wealth. Wouldn't
you give anything now just for a good hug?

March 23

NATURE ANYWAY

For Martín Prechtel

The air is clean and brisk, and the birds
have always insisted on social distancing.
And we can still walk out and do the same.

It's spring but the wind is cold, pushes
wrinkles across the face of the water.
Out on the river ducks, geese, mergansers,

buffleheads contribute heat to the great
warming of the seasons. Nature, anyway,
goes its way. Do you also have the feeling

that somehow it's wiser than we are,
that it knows, and is trying to show us,
something we don't? This is a sacred space

where whatever has died in us may yet
live. So don't succumb to complaining or
self-pity, just try to be present for it.

Putting no distance between yourself and
the earth, say *I'm ready for you to stand up
in me.* Say to the trees, *Make me the springtime.*

March 23

FIRST WEEK OF SPRING

Chickadee, redwing, robin give voice
to the force growing in the willows and oaks.
I can feel a palpable merriment
in the rain streaming down a riverbank,
the big bubbles excited to be bursting
into the flow that gives them wider life.

There's so much energy for us here
if we can just stand a moment and ask
the stones to push their steadiness up
toward our navel and the clouds to let down
a little of their buoyancy into our heart.
I love this time for the way astringent
and tender mix, to fill this old clay bowl
once more with the flavor of heaven.

March 26

APRIL

A textbook case of happiness

GOOD NEWS BELOW AND ABOVE

Trying to join heaven and earth in my mind,
I go out for a walk on the marshy
fringe of the lake. Life here is turned up
to full volume, Canada geese hissing
over their nesting places and the willows
shrill with red-wing blackbirds. I admire
so much the valiant young grass-blades
shouldering up through the dead winter mat,
the ground still damp with the last snow-melt.
Morning light falls so calmly into
the chasms in the bark of stiff old
cottonwoods carved with long care by the years.
And I think again of those faraway
events in gospel times and wonder
how I can make them real to myself
when suddenly a pair of sandhill cranes
fly over, two crosses on which no one
will die, sticking their necks out as all
prophets do, announcing to the world
in its moment of pain and fear a fresh
testament, laughing their kind of prayer.

April 6

YOUR EYES

When a certain slant of light, say from
a sunlit window, strikes the side of your face,
it catches your eye in such a way
as to call to my mind an early photo
your proud parents mailed out as a Christmas
greeting — you sitting in your tiny dress,
looking full at the world, not smiling but
inquisitive, alert. This picture has always
touched me for its intrinsic mystery
and beauty, but also for its strange capture
of some essence of you I've sensed but can't
quite grasp. For lovers it's unbearable
to have missed a single moment of
the beloved's life, but in your eyes
I seem to regain all that's been lost to time—
those blue eyes warm as waves on some ocean
beach. I stand in awe of their holiness
that grew from a cluster of starry cells
in your mother's womb, beautiful traveler
journeyed far to love and be loved in this world.

April 12

TINY POEM IN THE TAOIST MANNER

Happily writing poems
and practicing Qigong —
am I finally becoming the person
I used to think I was?

April 16

SMALL TURTLES SUNNING

Four turtles sun on a fallen trunk
a few feet from shore.
Painted turtles, the kind I used to catch
and keep for pets as a boy.
None larger than my spread hand,
their dark shells attract the light.
They stick their necks out
as far as they can to absorb the spring warmth —
what else can they do, clad
in all that stiff collar?
They spend so much of their lives
paddling the chill flow of the river,
chasing their shadows over the river bottom.
What a pleasure it must be for them
to seize a moment in the sun, let
the breeze rippling across the shallows dry their shells.
Though we're of the same tribe,
I'd prefer, when I go, to be an old tree
that turtles can climb up on to warm themselves.

April 20

FIRST EARTH DAY

It was a different country, a different earth –
Nixon had signed the Clean Air Act,
and we were still running on the fumes
of Woodstock the summer before.
Our senator Gaylord Nelson,
Wisconsin's pride, inaugurated
April 22nd as a day to honor the planet
(it should have been every day, every day).
I persuaded our student newspaper
to let me edit a supplement.
We all wrote for it, the new River Falls
Ecology Action, Jim, Phil, Eugene,
Margel and Dirty Bill, reprinted
Gary Snyder's "Smoky the Bear Sutra"
("may be reproduced free forever"),
for which Peggy crafted a marvelous
drawing of a globe-clutching Mother Earth
with her hand out, holding a car at bay.
It was a beautiful day for cleaning up
the Kinnickinnic; we hauled tires and bottles,
boots, a section of picket fence, and even
an old bed spring from the river behind
the movie theater! Hippies helped
police raise the flag in the park.
We sent big thanks and smiles to Mother Earth
that day, eight months after Woodstock,
and two weeks before the murders
at Kent State sent us all

back into the shadows,
still holding close the earth,
our sustenance, our mother, our lifeline.

April 21

BACK FENCE JAM

for Colin Cosgrove

It's social distancing time, and Colin
and I are having one of our jams
by the fence between our houses.
Colin is a music teacher just getting
started, and me, I'm trying not to
finish too soon. Colin is also
a bluegrass whiz on guitar and
mandolin, and we're out on a gorgeous
spring day playing and singing our hearts
out to the grass pushing up from below
and the budding trees exploding
in slow motion like green fireworks
against the clear blue sky. Colin
sings "The Old Home Place" and I sing
"Mountain Dew." Often we request
favorites of each other, and today
Colin asks for "Mr. Tambourine Man."
I'm always ready to oblige with that
Dylan masterpiece, all four verses,
and this time a male cardinal at the top
of a big basswood tree joins in. He's way
up there, warbling and trilling. I listen
for him to stop, but he doesn't.
He doesn't stop! He knows this song too
and keeps singing along. My God,
aren't we the trio! The neighbors' dogs,
meanwhile, are chasing each other
around their fenced-in yard, they're having
a good old time, rolling over on their

backs, feet kicking the air. Meanwhile
the cardinal, that red flame tipping
the highest branch like a candle,
is still trilling, and I want to stop
singing and yell to the world, "This is
a textbook example of happiness!"
so I do,

        then start singing again
because I don't want the cardinal to stop
and the song must go on, virus or no
virus, we must find ways to keep
singing together, even if only across
the back fence, and store such moments
away in our bones for those other days
sure to come, when we find ourselves
having to sing out against the silence.

April 24

EARTHWORMS IN THE RAIN

It's the first big rain of spring.
Puddles are full of earthworms,
stretched on the pavement,
some flattened, others slowly flexing
or curling in standing water.

I wonder how they come to drape
and festoon almost every square
foot of asphalt. How surprised
they must be, minding their own
business as aerators of the soil,
tiny agriculturists, helplessly
elevated by the flood into
however they experience light.

All of our carefully maintained
surfaces must be as full of holes
as a colander to let so many
of these pale workers up from
the planet's innards. Indeed,
Aristotle called them "the intestines
of the earth." The world we think
we know is only a skin over
the alive, teeming commons below.

Reserve for the many-hearted
earthworm the sympathy
you'd offer any farmer
unlucky enough to be lifted
by the whirlwind and set down
in the middle of rush hour traffic.

April 28

MAY

Life achieves her annual balance with death

GREEN IMMANENCE

April never gives us more than we can take.
May, now, that's another matter.
May comes on with her green that makes
us forget how somber the earth can be.
New leaves are a lime-green confetti thrown
up in the air, confetti that never
comes down. The occasion is every
event in your life that can possibly
be celebrated, all at once — wedding,
graduation, anniversary, birthday,
retirement — and it's all for you and
none of it is for you. The heart senses
something it has desired and feared, come near
and then draw back. And suddenly it's summer.

May 7

WILLOW STUMP BY THE SHORE

By the shore there's an old willow stump
about as big around as my arms' reach.
Apparently lifeless, the cracked and
hollowed barrel-like hulk has sent
up multiple new shoots that wave
in the cool May breeze. They are so light,
springy, and buoyant, no one would ever
think they'd proceeded from something as
over-and-done-with as the stump. Yet
here they are, greeting the world with all
the fresh optimism and energy
of any young life on this ancient earth.
So happy to be here, their slender
new flame-shaped leaves dancing in the sun!

May 12

TAPESTRY

We'll never grasp the moment of
spring's accomplishment, nor how
it was done, the new made again
out of the old recycled earth.
(We were like that once.)

Matter that has exhausted itself
in living, worked back into
the tapestry, the faded
fabric a warp upon which
the weft of the new is woven.

May 16

SQUINCHING

There was a short period, a few days
that felt longer for their uncertainty,
when, with few words at your disposal,
you communicated — those moments when
you were awake — by a series of
exaggerated, near-comic facial
expressions. I remember one in
particular where your eyes squinched
and mouth grimaced a kind of faux smile.

It was as if you were trying to squinch
yourself back to the life you'd left, with
effort wake yourself from the strange dream
of hospital beds, tests, and medications,
grimace it all away and come back
to your easier former self. All of this
I saw again this morning as you woke
safely back in our bed, grimacing, squinching
up from the grace of a normal sleep.

May 17

THE CRABAPPLE TREE

Overcast day, cool but with an edge of humidity. By now the green has closed ranks, high and low formed a united front against the crumbling ramparts of winter. Thus life achieves her annual balance with death and seems to rest today in that space between heartbeats.

The firs' new growth hangs in luxurious bright folds from their dark velvet sleeves. The buckeye holds aloft its thousand yellow candles. The limpid, sweet faces of the honeysuckle look on from their perfect collars of leaves. And that enormous pine that lost a branch to heavy spring snow the night of Lynn's retirement party saddens us with the memory of her death a few weeks later, the image of the girlish figure in the casket, all that was left of her woman's ampleness.

Near the edge of campus there's a crabapple tree whose blossom-laden branches cascade almost to the ground. The petals are a pale pink that makes us want to stand under it, so we do. It's a pink umbrella to keep out the gray rain. In our little bower, we are entirely enclosed by wheeling firmament, pink stars shining through the spokes of boughs. Here, clad in this falling gown of flowers, it's possible to remember every promise life makes to a young person in springtime.

i.m. Lynn Jermal

May 22

HAND IN POCKET

i.m. George Floyd

Remember Orwell's picture of the future
in *1984*? *Imagine a boot
stamping on a human face forever.*

Do Black people see in the footage
of Chauvin and Floyd *a white knee
crushing a black windpipe forever*?

The Black man's neck and shoulder are summer-
bare under the white cop's clothed knee. That should
tell you all you need to know about power.

Somehow almost worse is the cop's leisurely hand
in pocket. Why should that detail disturb us
so? As though the cop were doing nothing

more than rummaging for car keys. Floyd's
face is contorted while the cop retains
a flat, dispassionate composure. Murder

most casual . . . The Black man, soon to die, calling
for his mother, his cries for life and breath not enough
to roll the stone from the white cop's eyes.

May 30

JUNE

Summer singing at the top of its voice

THE PULSE

The leaves of oak, elm, and walnut
overhanging the shore pulse not with wind
but with continual gentle waves of light.
They are the lulling rays of summer
reaching us from the middle of the year,
which we sensed in winter faint as the pulse
of the very old. Now the light, stronger
each day, has us in its net, pulls us
toward the fullness of life. We could string
a hammock on this steep bank with its wild
phlox and honeysuckle and be rocked
by those bands of shade and shine passing
rhythmically over the leaves. And what is
causing these emanations? Sun flashing
from the placid rings rippling outward
from the mother wood duck and her four
ducklings out on the windless river.

June 1

MASKS

Behind my mask I smile at you.
Behind your mask you smile at me.
A mask covers a small part of us.
It's not only with our mouths
we smile, but with our whole bodies.
I can tell whether you like me
even when you're wearing a mask.
I think you can tell whether I like you
even when I'm wearing a mask.
To keep us from coming apart,
we'll need to let our smiles roam
out past the edges of our distances.
Is there a way our masks might
make us a little less afraid to love?

June 6

THE ICE FISHERMAN

Like everyone, he complained of the long northern winters but didn't really mind them. During the cold, dark months he could be found hunched over a hole punched in a Minnesota lake, out in the open, sitting on an overturned pail, squinting into the flat, glaring distance or on a bench in some shack comfortable with failure, darkness serving to illuminate the circular window below. This was the life of the poet, not so different, from the life of a bear, both dependent in their ways on foraging, fishing prowess and luck. Shy forms hovered just out of sight of that hole, introverted, undemonstrative Midwestern fish. And he knew better than almost anyone how to reel them in on the bait of laughter.

i.m. Louis Jenkins

June 17

THE LONG SUMMER

Nineteenth of June. It's going to be a long
summer. All of our seasonal celebrations
cancelled or gone virtual, home-bound,
the question becomes what to do with the space
we confront when we turn away from
our devices. Does our time explode
or implode? There are abysses in
the hours we take pains to avoid,
whole emotional Mariana Trenches
of memory and apprehension that can
be worked around only by staying
insanely busy. For some this way
indeed lies madness, spreading
from the top like venom from a snakebite.
But others, it's likely, may look back
on this as the summer that stretched beyond
the parentheses of Memorial Day
and Labor Day to become a world
unto itself in which we rediscovered
and perhaps were able to keep for a while
the riches of expanse and dreaming
we'd so often and yearningly recalled
but failed to grasp, glimpse them as we might
in the clouded playroom mirror of childhood.

June 19

SUMMER YARD QIGONG

For Colleen Gray

Music wraps around us, the *scree*
of a jay, a sunset robin, other
less identifiable singers, set
against the backdrop of a rain-
swollen river surging over falls.
What is Qi if not all of these,
and the breathing moistness of grass
under our bare feet and the immense
arching of the black walnut
overhead? We gather it up,
take the world-medicine into
our blood and bones, become
truly a part of the living earth,
a more conscious vessel for
the beautiful energies to surge
through, as the river, fattened
with seven inches of rain, carries
all the exhilaration of summer
singing at the top of its voice.

June 30

JULY

In wonder and hunger before the
Gates of Paradise

LIGHTHOUSE

So much has happened to us and around
us since Christmas, surgeries and viruses,
so much has changed in us and in the world,
we might easily forget if we didn't
take special care to remember that,
fear and turmoil notwithstanding, today
is the anniversary of that first
morning we woke together in the same
bed and found in our love a lighthouse
throwing its beam over the waves of our lives
to guide us home on seas placid or
stormy to this sun-lit harbor in a
summer land where hearts seek shelter and
come at last to anchor in each other.

July 4

ANGER IN THE TIME OF COVID

At the city yard waste site I heft
sodden leaf bags from the back of our car.
They've sat on the lawn too long, killed
square yards of grass where I piled them.
Others are driving up to unload their
grass trimmings and tree branches. I'm jumpy
when someone pulls up too near, feel a twinge
of something like cold anger that takes me
aback. Is this who I want to be?
Is this who the times are making me?
A perfectly friendly man has stopped
to see what's been dragging under his car
(a slender stick). Driving home, I notice
three younger people, in their twenties
I'd guess, gathered too close around the back
of a pickup, none of them wearing masks.
A handsome young man is laughing. I feel
fear for him, and then the anger again
at this group's lack of self-protection.
But I'd be lying if I didn't also
say that I feel some envy for the easy
camaraderie of youth these blithe
ignorers are enjoying. Oh, young strangers,
be well in these times I fear are starving
our most basic human sympathies!

July 11

A HAPPY LIFE

For Dr. James Iwakiri

Two months past my surgery, I walk
with Krista on a July morning.
It's the heart of summer, flowers festive
with color — yellow trefoil, purple harebells,
lavender bergamot, orange day lilies —

the black raspberries coming ripe, for which
we stop often along the path to redden
our fingers with their tart sweets, succulent
with the past days' rain. The dread doesn't go
away, but neither does it weight this joy.

The sky is radiant. A jay lights on
a fence post as if to lead the way.
I'm still me, to borrow a quip from Lee
Hayes, more or less. Even in the best
of times, no one knows what will happen next.

We can only learn to rest on the present
moment. Isn't that bread "sufficient
unto the day"? A happy life is always
here, waiting for us to discover it,
ripening among the brambly hours.

July 15

NEOWISE

Seen from the bridge at half-past ten,
you're a faint brush-stroke on the shifting
margin of evening. Where the semi-dark turns
into deeper dark, you hang in motionless
motion, half-seen, half-intuited.

Broomstraw of the night! Hard to believe
that this delicate specter, head and tail
fine as a wind-blown cottonwood seed,
is a three-mile-wide ice ball hurtling
into view every sixty-eight hundred years.

July 17

SUMMER GARDEN

If we can be said to have a garden, it's an uncultivated
one. Bee balm, phlox, and lilies, none of which we
planted, spread out from the south side of the house,
claiming more of the yard each summer.

This evening we stand on a narrow strip of lawn
between two fragrant patches of red, orange, pink, and
white, some almost head-high, and watch the lowering
sun illuminate layer upon layer of black walnut leaves,
ember making the whole world-hearth glow.

We are not alone. A hummingbird hangs in flight,
backlit, its wings a transparency pinned to air. A
hummingbird hawk-moth sips among the phlox, sampling
with its proboscis the flushed blossoms, living to the
fullest its few weeks on earth. A bumblebee bobs among
the low crimson streamers of bee balm.

I would take every one of these into myself, to store
against the great vacancy of winter. And who knows
whether they may not survive in some way the crossing
to that farther shore? Maybe there they won't tear my
heart as they do here with their fugitive abundance, their
gratuitous beauty, here where I walk on a summer's early
evening among the throngs of phlox against the backdrop
of sunset and know that I am again standing in wonder
and hunger before the gates of Paradise.

July 23

71

AUGUST

World-sky flooded with light

A KINGFISHER

*Who conceived the eye back in the primeval darkness of
early evolution?*

—Guy Murchie, *The Seven Mysteries of Life*

A kingfisher's white neck band flashes,
spot of brightness among the dusky trees.
Fascinating to watch his fishing
ritual, abrupt nosedive into
the water, completely vanishing
before splashing up and outward back
into the trees with a little cackle
of — what? satisfaction? disappointment?
joy? — to scan again for swimming prey.
If I stand here long enough I'll see him
dive, splash and rise again in his swooping
flight. Lucky us, to have eyes able
to zoom in on a hectic flier across
a river. Luckier still his own many
times more acute vision for those quick
scattering lives on which he subsists.
I don't doubt that were the whole earth blind
we'd have other equally vivid ways
of perceiving, but that would be
a different universe. So let's give
thanks for this world-sky flooded with light
for all the sighted beings, a gift from
the divine, unseen creator of eyes.

August 1

FORGIVING OUR BODIES

Have I forgiven my body for growing older?
Have I forgiven my hair for quitting
its job of shading my scalp from the sun?
My back for declining to lift the weights it used to?
My teeth for politely foregoing their former
diet of hard and tough morsels?
Have I forgiven my longevity genes for refusing to let me
"live fast, die young, and leave a beautiful corpse"?

Have I forgiven the inward parts of myself
that will gradually lose their ability to play
a reliable role in the intricate drama
of my body, those organs whose eventual
failure we so easily view as a betrayal
in the final act by a rogue actor?

Having forgiven them,
may I then rest in the grace of aging
and know that by no malevolence
of myself or the universe this is how
we ebb as the vast tide pulls our wave back out to sea.

While you have time, while you have breath,
forgive yourself most deeply, and don't forget
to ask forgiveness of the parts of yourself
you have wronged and betrayed through carelessness and
    ignorance.
We have all been too careless, taken
too much for granted this magnificent horse
upon which our earthly life is mounted,
though that too seems to have been part of the ride.

August 4

76

BRIGHT PORTAL

On a late summer morning the walk-
way turns through dappled shade toward
the east where the sun's dazzle on
the river breaks through and dissolves the path
forward in light as though a luminous
tunnel has suddenly opened into the trees.
Could that bright portal be offering
a glimpse of the pathway by which we
walk out of this life? The radiance is so
intense it's not hard to imagine
it as a congeries of beloved faces
pressing near in greeting — so glad
to see us again — those we'd thought lost
coming to guide us back to a time
that is not earth time, a placeless place
where we've been together all along.

August 14

CEDAR WAXWINGS

This morning I thought, *Summer's*
almost over and I still haven't seen
any waxwings. Now I'm standing at
one of my favorite spots on the river
shore and here they are, grinning
their joy through their little black
bandit masks, flitting and cavorting
in their clowning manner. Always in groups,
always keeping up their aerobatics
as if for nothing more than the joy of it,
looping and diving among the willows
overhanging the water, never staying
in one place long. Sometimes the crests
standing up on their buffy heads
seem to shiver in wild delight,
one of those worlds Blake saw closed
by our "senses five." Grateful
to have found them again, I open wide
my heart's healing sky to let in
their crazybird air show medicine.

August 20

VULNERABILITY

I drove her to the ER, followed
the ambulance to the city, practically
lived at the hospital while sleeping alone
in our house the whole three months the stroke
took her away from home. What I didn't
learn until later, as she recovered,
was that once you've seen someone in their
vulnerability your relationship
with them can never be the same. Some
firewall of protection goes down, and then
you must step forward to be her shield,
her defender against the dangers,
and, loving her, find that she's become even
more precious to you than she was before.

August 28

SEPTEMBER

Have I only now learned how to love

ORB WEAVER

There it was, deep in the Kinnickinnic
woods, hovering like a smoke ring
where young maple and young elm
contended for space so that it was
impossible to tell just where
it was anchored, where mottled
morning sun struck through
to light it: at first I absurdly
thought someone had strung a CD
in the trees, so round and prismatic
it appeared in its suspension,
or more absurdly a hologram
of a CD, flimsy, shimmering, yet
dimensional, as the sun above and
behind fired red and gold tones
into its close concentric grooves.
At last recognizing it for what
it was, I could make out the bright
bead of the orb weaver's body
working in meticulous circles
inward toward the empty center,
that perfectly round nothing,
so accommodating and yielding
to the fine intensity
of her plan, her craft.

September 6

PLEASE FORGIVE ME

This morning, preparing a breakfast with
oyster mushrooms from Ed and Jenelle's woods,
I felt a momentary stab of annoyance
when you abruptly abandoned our
task to peel garlic cloves to add
to beans for tonight's soup-making.

Immediately the memory rushed in
of your painstaking attempt in OT
barely six months ago to make
a PB&J sandwich, trying so hard
to put the scattered pieces of ordinary
routine back together. A grief I'd
mostly kept at bay since last spring came over
me then at the sight of your managing
so normally in our kitchen, regret
for my reflexive impatience.

Among my complicated, strong
emotions the only words
I could find were those I found hard
to presently speak: Please
forgive my forgetting, even
for an instant, your effortful
courage-steps, beginning again.

September 13

RED SUN RISING

Sun shouldn't be this red this high.
It's a wrong beauty. Smoke-plumes
across the continent from burning Oregon,
burning California tint our sunrise
a sunset. Our river banded
summer-algae green sparkles copper.
All day a pinkish eye will sear
a furrow in the dirty blue.

Out west, the sky bends and
buckles, a sheeted flame from
the lit match of earth, orange
as the grotesquely made-up face
of the arsonist to whom the forests
are entrusted—American sundown.

September 15

THE CHILL

Burst from the low trees along the path,
bird resolves to *hawk*, and in a flash
of vision, the little load it carries
in its claws a smaller bird. Oh Red-Tail,
so admired by us when perched on a fence-
post beside the highway, you also are
prey to larger raptors, as evidenced
by the surgically detached bundle of
rusty tail-feathers we found not far
from here, trimmed away from the meat of the bird.
This is the chill of the nature we love,
the occasionally glimpsed fact. Somber
overcast, earth cooling, the leaves' cover
soon to be blown, leaving many exposed.

September 15

CALLING IT

Just to see and hear him on a screen
hurts the soul. Stench of abuse.
The Abyss hijacks the microphone,
no muting the rant the psychotic
can't switch off in his head.

The assault on truth is visceral:
the viewer's knees tremble, breath comes
up short. Lies fly out of the mouth
in black streams. They are his children:
father of lies, lord of the flies.

Damaged horror child exposed.
The networks call it a "debate."
Burroughs called it "naked lunch."
Yeats called it "rough beast." I call it
"rape in an abandoned house."

September 30

THE PAPER PUZZLE

Last winter in rehab at Courage
Kenny, Rec Therapy had you work on
a sticker-by-number puzzle, gray and
black paper pieces that resolve
into a kind of cubist version of a
famous early portrait of the Beatles.
Six months home, sorting papers,
you find it again. I recall
accidentally glimpsing it in
the hospital: you'd thought to give it as
a valentine, but the element
of surprise was blown. Today you're driving again
and doing most things you could before
the stroke, even finishing the puzzle,
for fun and perhaps for remembrance.
It's not as easy as it looks, still
only half-done, many irregular
numbered spaces still awaiting
their tiny stickers.
                         It's hard to believe that
any of this happened, that the mind and
hands that planned and executed
intricate beaded baskets had to learn
coordinated cognition all over
again by way of simple tasks
like this sticker puzzle. Was I ever
afraid you wouldn't come back all the way?
We all were, which is why seeing you now
so whole seems such a miracle. But
I know also with a fierce certainty

that I would have loved equally however
much or little of you made the return
trip home. Somehow — I still don't under-
stand it — we traveled together to that
"edge of doom" and, holding hands in the void,
waited out the night. I vow to not
forget our desperate winter and the many
who helped and prayed us through it. Have I only now
learned how to love? We are more careful
with each other and with ourselves.
Your paper puzzle, remnant of that
season of unknowing, reminds me how fragile
it all really is, and all of the time —
yet how supported we are, how safe —
and how you are your own best Valentine.

September 30

OCTOBER

The longing we feel for the lost good to return

TRIO

There's a straight line from Mars
down to the cricket song on the corner.

Mars, lone red flashpoint in the early
October evening, a world apart.

Unseen cricket making solitary
sounds in the long grass in the dark.

And I, third point on the triangle,
measuring my distance from both.

"What is it, then, between us?" Walt
asked famously. I wish I knew.

I stand here thinking about the cricket,
its rickety insistence,

the planet's steady point of light,
the bluer light we make in space.

Cricket, are you hopeful or merely
persistent? Planets die, too.

What *is* it, then, between us
three amigos, worlds apart?

October 6

JOHN RESTORED

Well, John, you'd have turned eighty today,
as fine a fall day as we see in these parts,
a day to make one pity the dead
missing this splurge of heavenly gold.
What are we to make of this birthday
that forty years ago became an anniversary?

What's to say that hasn't been said already?
"Nothing you can say, but you can learn how
to play the game"? Is that what we're left with?
Your death resists sense and for that matter
so does your life. It was a gift, and gifts
aren't to be made sense of, they're to be
accepted. Just as faithfully as the unseen
immune defenses in our bodies, your
songs will go on protecting and healing.
They're part of our spiritual body now,
the world immune system that is always
moving to act against threats of the times.

Near the end of the film *Yesterday*,
that fantasy of a world that has lost
its collective memory of the Beatles,
the protagonist drives out to a cottage
near the sea, presumably near
Liverpool. The camera pans slowly
past windows, tantalizes with glimpses
of oddly familiar drawings
inside: an artist lives here. When our
hero knocks, the aging man who comes
to the door is unmistakably

John Lennon, an older John who, by
being forgotten by the world has been
therefore allowed to live. That moment
shocks the film deeper, touches the longing
we feel for the lost good to return.
And here he is, straight out of that heart
of longing, John restored to the elder
we dream he might actually have become,
seasoned by the wisdom of that half-
lifetime taken from him. No way to know
who he'd have finally turned out, what gifts
still to be given from new self-knowledge.
Who knows where they'd have gone together,
who knows what future they'd have crafted,
two artists who'd mastered the everyday
art of starting over? On this day
when, John Ono Lennon, you'd have turned
eighty, we can only imagine.

October 9

BASSWOOD LEAVES

On our 35th wedding anniversary

October is hasting toward November.
More sky now, more room for light to get in.
The basswood drops its great heart-shaped leaves
on the path, each a Valentine at our feet.
Why do I feel so certain that they fall
without regret, without sadness, that
instead they're love-notes from the earth? This is
the season of revelation. Our vision
less occluded, we see better what
was always there, hidden in plain sight,
which we've hidden from ourselves. Can it
be that the soul does not grieve but loves
this fall-time for the joy of what it will
make next from the art materials
of this world? Is it an artist in us
who sings through the melancholy of autumn
leaves? Just as the basswood tree will bring
back its heart-shaped leaves, surely some branch
on the tree of the universe will know
how to make a heart like yours, a heart like mine.

October 19

ON THE EVE OF ANOTHER COVID WINTER

A late October snow is falling.
Once I wrote, "I'm more interested
in what we keep than what we lose."
We know that much is being lost,
more will be lost in the coming
winter. Can I rise above my
own losses? What is it we keep?

Let gratitude be our guide now.
Start with the face of the person
nearest you. The walls holding in
warmth, keeping out cold. Carpet
of autumn leaves unrolling you a path.
Your good heart. Your awake, alive mind.
Questions falling like October snow.

October 23

GEESE MANEUVERS

At the cross-quarter. Clouds decide how much brightness to allot to earth. Some light manages to straggle through, silver the river on which hundreds of Canada geese gather. Each is a dark Arthurian craft magicked here by the primordial imagination of the universe.

They are in a state of dynamic flow — one moment their slender-prowed silhouettes rest at anchor, then become a field in motion toward a common point. From relative calm an agitation builds, from quiet a surround of voices noisy as a canyon full of barking dogs. All face in the same direction until, given some crucial signal, their clamor reaches a furious pitch and they cyclone upward, tearing off pieces of the river with their wings and feet. Squadrons appear to rehearse migratory protocols, flock downstream only to circle back again to the settling water. It's a mystery who commands these maneuvers and how others know to join: "I'm ready!" "Me too!" "I'm in!" "Let's go!"

It can be hypnotic, this surging energy, rhythmic as the breathing of an immense lung. We could stand all day and watch their comings and goings, tumultuous departures and returns to the endlessly accommodating river.

October 30

NOVEMBER

*No reason to believe we'll be
abandoned now*

SUNSET IN NOVEMBER

Evenings come earlier in November.
Leaves no longer shield our vision from
the setting sun. There's something so exposed
in the way the red-hot light bulbs down
into black trees, enters the horizon.
We know we could not be so confident,
so bold. We are for small fires and comforts,
not that head-first dive into darkness.
Have we been too timid lovers then?
Have we not brought enough ardor, enough
courage to our loves? Well, we're past the point
of no return, youthful strength and daring
behind us. We must hope to ride another
kind of love into the night sky like a moon.

November 3

THE ELECTION CALLED FOR BIDEN

Mild early November, arterial branches
saturated in late afternoon light.
Pale leaves still clinging to distant trees
give an illusion of springtime. The sun
is a golden yolk whisked with the white
of cirrus clouds in the sky-kettle.

This morning I stood in the park with others
rallying for fair districting maps, then greeted
musician friends playing by the river.
Around eleven the news came over
someone's phone. Passing cars honked approval —
all our faces freshly flushed with hope.

Many things suddenly become possible.
Dreams spring new again like winter wheat.

November 7

FIRST AID KITS

After less than two weeks in our house,
our three-month-old kittens, Violet and Lou,
like, maybe even love, and accept us
into their tiger tribe. Black Violet,
tuxedo Lou, stretch on their round white bed,
lie with bellies and paws up, evident
posture of vulnerability and trust.
In a time when most of us fear for our
bodies, they display casual beauty,
magnificence in the flesh. The healing
they bring is no small gift. I must have conquered
some cruelty in myself to have become
capable of this closeness. Just their wanting
to be near is a kind of medicine.

Wild as they roll together into one
indistinguishable ear-biting, hind-leg-
kicking ball or, spent, dozing sweetly
on a lap, they fill every vacant nook
with presence. We'll not miss this moment
of our cats' childhood, which anyway
still goes by too fast. Barring disasters,
they'll be the companions of our old age,
settled as us, these diminutive whirlwinds
that already shadow our every step,
requiring us to walk carefully, fondly.
Let the days slow and stretch for the four
hearts beating under this roof. We are all
in love and there's nowhere we need to go.

November 12

WHAT HAPPENED LAST WINTER

A blindness had come over me, and it
seemed I was bound to fall into a hole.
That was a dark hole in the heart of winter,
where it sometimes felt as though sleep was my
only refuge. But morning always brought some
provisional light. I got back behind
the wheel, and enough small packets of help
arrived that I knew we had not been
forsaken. Seized and shaken, yes, but not
forgotten, and not alone. Life can be
less than gentle with you in its jaws
when you've missed instructions to change and grow.
You'll have to say what's true for you; I can
only speak for myself. I had known it was
coming for a long time, and this is when it happened.
While you, dear, one, were learning to walk again
I was learning a harder kind of loving.

November 25

NOON, THANKSGIVING

The sun far enough south now that it throws
the entire shadow of the neighbors' house
onto the street, in a way one never sees
when leaves are on the trees and the sun
higher in the sky. We are entering
the pared-down world where what was hidden
is revealed, where shadows claim their rightful
place. And there are shadows we don't see
even on Thanksgiving, the damage we do
through lack of gratitude, consecration
of grievance. Every day we don't get down
on our knees and thank the earth is wasted.
We should be more than just the shadow of
a house falling, chilling the hard pavement.

November 27

ADVENT CANDLE: HOPE

Wind shakes bare branches against darkening
clouds. The garden whirligig dances madly
on the graves of the phlox. We know now
how shock can enter the seasons, and
how precious each day able and upright
in this world of trouble. Hope is the candle
we light beginning again the new
journey, come round again, from death into
rebirth of the year, the celebration
of the holy child inextricably bound
to the ritual dismissal of the ancient
we feel sorry for, his promise outworn
if not betrayed. Strike a match — there is still
much for which to be grateful as we stand
together in the evergreen circle.
We have many steps yet to take,
many miles yet to travel into the dark
and the light, and absolutely no reason
to believe we'll be abandoned now.

November 29

DECEMBER

A year when we didn't die

LITTERMATES

Their bodies are so beautiful, sunlight
through the window striking brownish tints in
their glossy black fur. Naturally regal,
they stretch in luxurious languor,
soft limbs intertwined in a way not yet
quite sexual. Doing every moment
exactly as their nature dictates,
they're two perfect young beings sharing
a closeness only littermates know.
They can streak, black lightning, across the floor
or rest in balanced calm, two sets of peaked
ears alert, in their favorite chair.
Imagine how the world comes new to them
their first winter, how mischievous the snow.

December 2

ADVENT CANDLE: PEACE

Peace to the goose with the broken wing, eliciting
    the maddening kindness of human beings, maddening
    because inconsistently applied.
Peace to the snapping turtle burrowed in the river bottom
    mud, frozen and sealed as if for Judgment Day.
Peace to the queen bee in her hive, kept warm
    at the center of a ball made of thousands of her
    subjects, not all of whom will survive the winter.
Peace to the bear in her leafy den, giving birth
    in her sleep, as it seems that poets sometimes do,
    astonished to awaken to the bright, hungry eyes
    of the poem.
Peace to the trees keeping their minds on heaven,
    while holding fast the under-sky of roots and mycelia.
Peace to the clouds, shielding the sun from the
    glaring follies of humans below.
Peace to all the fevered world with its rising
    tempers and tides.
Peace to the famished who have eaten the poisoned
    bread of lies.
Peace to the strangers to themselves, unable to abide
    their own company.
Peace to those from whom everything has been stripped,
    who shiver in fear of the coming winter,
    having never recovered from the last.
Peace to those who live in dread of the picture
    the puzzle pieces of dusk are assembling.
Peace to those whom anger and shame keep awake
    through the long night, fighting the reckoning
    that collapses the day.

Peace to the one who lights a single candle, hoping its heat
    is enough to keep him alive while help is on its way.
Peace to those who wait patiently and impatiently
    for a new song to be born in the silence.

December 8

MID-DECEMBER MORNING

A chickadee sings the pre-solstice sun
edging along the southern horizon.
After days of overcast, the light is
spreading its fingers in the constricted
spaces within us. It's a joy to stride
freely in the open air and breathe the freshness
of approaching winter. Many creatures
already burrow into their sleep
hidden by earth. Are we then the lucky
ones to wake with only a middling hunger
as the year drops to its nadir? We walk
in bright mystery, like that prismatic
wisp of cloud west of the sun, lit as though
a runway for an arriving angel.

December 17

ADVENT CANDLE: JOY

December past its mid-point and only days
until our dreaded anniversaries.
It's seven in the morning. Every Friday
at this hour the classical station plays
Handel's "Happy We" chorus and we dance.
Rock and roll and swing and square dance cross
in our kitchen improvisations,
a hundred seconds of high spirits before
we lapse back into our sleepy breakfasting.
And I think, if last Christmas we'd been
permitted just one glimpse of us
here, a year on, doing as we've always done,
how that would have eased our fears and lightened
our spirits. But that was a job for faith,
who gave no such assurances, only an
amazingly dogged trust in future joy,
her one fierce candle in that winter dark.

December 18

WINTER SOLSTICE CONJUNCTION

when I hear this kind of song

—Amy Rigby, "Bob"

Tonight the rare conjunction of Saturn
and Jupiter, as not observable
from earth since the year 1226 . . .
Maybe a greater wonder than their proximity
in our view is this occasion on which
it falls, the winter solstice — what were
the odds of that, not to mention our being
alive to see it? Ravenous senex
and jovial giant locked tonight
in their binary waltz on the dance
floor of the sky while the orchestra
of the spheres plays its old ambivalent
music to the groundlings in the pit:
happy/sad   happy/sad   happy/sad

December 21

ADVENT CANDLE: LOVE

You'd collapsed, still dressed, on my side of
the bed, your back turned to me. *Wrong wrong wrong*
rang the alarm in my brain as I strained

to budge you awake. "Aren't you supposed
to go in to work this morning?" "I guess
so," you said listlessly. It was eight a.m.

As I struggled your arms into the coat
you looked me straight in the eye and said
spacily, "You're freaking out." "Fucking

right I'm freaking out!" I said, panicking.
"We've got to go!" That morning Love became
a soldier in the winter trenches of

a war he'd never expected to fight.
My newly installed night bag emptied
and hooked onto a belt-loop under

my coat, I tried not to make a spectacle
of myself at the ER, though the nurse
admitting you assured me they'd seen it

all before. Suddenly we were no longer
on the planet we'd known, cast-offs cut loose
from our familiar lives, set adrift.

Like space-walking astronauts, we faced
an enveloping void, yet somehow remained
tethered to the mother ship of a force

greater than ourselves that even in
the absolute zero between worlds
would not let us escape its gravity.

Loving you more than I could love myself
was the single candle-flame kindling
the star that kept me alive that Christmas.

December 24

WHO HEALS

Who heals, and who is healed?

I don't want to wish this year
over because it was
a year when we didn't die.
Anyway it's unwise
to wish away your time.

Think of those who said "Good
riddance" to 2019.
We walk the road of this
moment between the best
and worst we can imagine.

We don't know what lies
waiting up ahead,
but we do know that
we're not unaccompanied,
not without help.

There are healers
both within and without us
of whom we know nothing.
The intensity of their
light can be frightening.

How would it feel
to whole-heartedly wish
ourselves well, be willing
to doctor the parts of
ourselves that make us sick?

Do we have the courage
to stand up to the voices
that tell us there is
only bad luck, loss,
a horrible end?

Do we have the courage
to be kind to our past,
forgive the mis-steps
that have led to the cliff's edge
from which we back away?

Can it be we're afraid
of knowing ourselves so powerful?
If only we could trust
the way we've come so far,
and answer the questions:

Who is healed, and who heals?

December 31

Epilogue: 2021

YELLOW FERRIS WHEEL

In the dream it was summer. Luxury of freedom from winter clothes and green of treetops burgeoning beyond the storefronts on Main Street. The town swarming with high-spirited crowds in a holiday mood. The naturalness of it seemed unaccountably strange, as if the old life had passed into myth and those mythic times reborn. Suddenly I understood it was our city's annual summer festival returned after last year's cancellation. Rides were going up, and right here in the downtown supermarket's parking lot carnies were erecting a bright yellow Ferris wheel, its paint new, shiny, glazed in sunlight. I exclaimed to Krista, "Oh, it must be over!" And so it was: No masks, no fear, no physical distancing. There was something of childhood in our happiness over those yellow spokes growing toward the sky.

January 1

TWELFTH NIGHT

I've always loved what that mad boy Rimbaud
called "Christmas on the earth," by which he meant
a sense of the holy that does not pass.
There are wise souls in us who have never
given up following the star. It would
be a shame to deny them for fear
of what foolish people might say.
Since we can no longer take for granted
the simple fact of our being here
together, let's play the old Christmas
records once more, raise our glasses to
the astonishing fidelity of
the Marvelous that every year we live
makes of the willing heart a manger
in the cold, dark Palestines of winter.

January 5

NOTES ON THE POEMS

"'You'll Never Walk Alone'": The video cited in the poem can easily be found on YouTube. At least as moving is a short video about the radio project described in the poem, posted with my poem when it appeared online at the British *International Times* site: internationaltimes.it/youll-never-walk-alone/

"Good News Below and Above": This poem was written on April 6th at the beginning of Holy Week in anticipation of Easter Sunday on the 12th. I have long written Christmas poems, but Easter poems are relatively new for me; I'm still feeling my way into the deeper spirit of that season.

"Back Fence Jam": You can hear and view a song Colin and I recorded between our back yards in April, 2020, with the help of my wife Krista, at https://www.youtube.com/watch?v=0A4is-xbsCY. Here we subject the Pete Seeger/Lorre Wyatt composition "God's Counting on Me, God's Counting on You" to the "folk process," adding a couple of our own verses tailored to COVID times.

"The Crabapple Tree": This poem remembers our beloved friend, the artist and educator Dr. Lynn Jermal at the University of Wisconsin - River Falls. Lynn died at age 59 in 2012.

"The Ice Fisherman": This poem honors the great Minnesota poet Louis Jenkins, who died on winter solstice in 2019. Almost every American poet who writes prose poems owes him a debt. I tried to capture a little of Louis's wry Midwestern humor in this tribute.

"Summer Yard Qigong": My title has some fun ringing local changes on Master Chunyi Lin's Minnesota-based Spring Forest Qigong. In warm weather my wife and I practice in our yard with our friend, Colleen Gray, who studied with Master Lin.

"NEOWISE": Comet NEOWISE was a spectral visitor to our skies mostly in July, 2020, the brightest comet visible in the northern hemisphere since Hale-Bopp in 1997. It will return in 6,800 years.

"A Kingfisher": The epigraph of this poem is from a marvelous book by Guy Murchie called *The Seven Mysteries of Life*. Murchie, a brilliant polymath, spent 17 years trying to understand the whole of the natural world. Published in 1978, *Seven Mysteries* still packs more amazement per page than any other book I know. Definitely one of my "desert island" picks.

"Calling It": Written following the ominous televised presidential debate on September 29. The second debate, scheduled for October 15, was canceled due to one candidate's COVID diagnosis and refusal to appear remotely, a relief to many viewers.

"Advent Candle: Hope": I have long written poems for the Christmas holiday, but little for Advent. I resolved to write a poem for each of the weekly themes of Advent,

Hope, Peace, Joy, and Love; the results form a kind of framework for this last stretch of the book.

"Mid-December Morning": In some of its details of how animals survive winter, this poem (as well as "Advent Candle: Peace") draws on Gayle Boss's poignant, poetic book *All Creation Waits: The Advent Mystery of New Beginnings* (2016).

"Winter Solstice Conjunction": Both the epigraph and last line quote the touching song "Bob" from Amy Rigby's 2018 CD *The Old Guys*.

ACKNOWLEDGMENTS
AND THANKS

Several of these poems were originally published in the following online journals: *Grey Sparrow Journal, International Times* (UK, online), *New Verse News* (online), and *Poetrybay* (online).

"Back Fence Jam," "Hand in Pocket," "The Loneliness" and "'You'll Never Walk Alone'" appeared in my 2020 collection *Storm Island* from Red Dragonfly Press. It was one of the last books to be published by that true Renaissance man Scott King, whose early death I mourn.

"Basswood Leaves" and "Orb Weaver" first appeared in *Ekphrasis: A Sister Arts II Exhibit of Poetry and Visual Arts* at the Phipps Center for the Arts in Hudson, Wisconsin, and in the accompanying book, edited by Lee Kisling, Lana Sjoberg, and Margaret Welshons.

A few of these poems were reprinted in *Poems of Hope and Reassurance* and *More Poems of Hope and Reassurance* edited by Lina Belar and appeared on the Green Island Poetry Walk in Wadena, Minnesota.

"Lighthouse" appeared in *Startled by Love 2021: New Poems in Traditional Forms*, edited by Laura Vosika.

"Green Immanence" and "Willow Stump by the Shore" appeared in *Startled by Nature 2020: New Poems in Traditional Forms*, edited by Laura Vosika.

"Anger in the Time of COVID" and "The Long Summer" appeared in *21st Century Plague: Poetry from a Pandemic*, edited by Elayne Clift.

Many thanks to the editors for permission to reprint.

Finally, big thanks to my publisher Julie Pfitzinger for her enthusiastic encouragement and support. Many thanks to my friend the poet and baker Danny Klecko for steering me to Paris Morning. And I thank artist John Ilg for his evocative cover art perfectly fitting the mood of this book. Thanks too to fellow poets Patrick Cabello Hansel, Margaret Hasse, and Danny Klecko for their back-cover recommendations.

While Western medicine has played a central role in our recoveries, Krista and I have also been grateful recipients of medicines from varied traditions. Important healings from Asian, Native American, and Judeo-Christian cultural streams have all come at critical moments. Throughout, our wider community in River Falls, Wisconsin stepped up mightily to support us financially, spiritually and emotionally. Reader, may you never need to draw on community resources in this way, but if you do, I hope you live somewhere as caring and generous as our town. You never really know how supported you are until you find yourself in crisis as we did that winter of 2019-20.

Krista and I have many friends and healers to thank. A very partial list must include:

Western medicine: Dr. Ganesh Asaithambi, Mary Carlson, Dr. Amy Chai, Dr. James Kolbeck, Dr. Derek Nelson, Dr. David Prall, Dr. Amy Schreiner, Dr. Timothy Steinmetz, Dr. Greg Stern, Dr. Carrie Torgersen, Val Zellmer, and the brilliant and skilled Dr. James Iwakiri.

Deepest thanks to the dedicated caring staff at these three facilities where Krista was treated: United Hospital, St. Paul, Minnesota; Courage Kenny Rehabilitation Institute, St. Paul, Minnesota; and Kinnic Health and Rehabilitation, River Falls, Wisconsin. My personal thanks to the kind staff of the Oak Leaf Surgical Hospital in Eau Claire, Wisconsin.

Eastern medicine: Master Gadu Doushin, Emily Jacobson, Dr. Roger Jahnke, Master Chunyi Lin, Master Jerry Wellik, and the timely gift of Spring Forest Qigong's teachers daily Facebook practice. Special gratitude to Ruth Bly who suggested Qigong to me and Colleen Gray, our neighbor and Qigong master.

Indigenous medicine: We owe more than we can express to our incomparable friend, the Mayan healer Martín Prechtel. Thirteen thank-you's! Thanks also for a healing breathing practice taught by Russell Four Eagles.

More friends than I can list here have lent generous support in food and money donations, and in other essential kinds of help in a difficult time. Together you helped us avoid serious medical debt. We'll never forget you. Special mention should be made of the outpouring of generosity from Spirit of Grace Church, then led by pastor Amy DeLong, a great ally to us in our crises. Thanks also to our families for their assistance, especially sister Sandy

Spieler who was there whenever I couldn't be, and vice versa.

Thanks lastly and always to our mother Earth whose health is our health. These poems were written on land shared by the Dakota and Ojibway peoples. No war is known to have been fought here.

ABOUT THE AUTHOR

Thomas R. Smith is author of ten books of poems, *Keeping the Star (*New Rivers Press, 1988), *Horse of Earth* (Holy Cow! Press, 1994), *The Dark Indigo Current* (Holy Cow! Press, 2000), *Winter Hours* (Red Dragonfly Press, 2005), *Waking Before Dawn* (Red Dragonfly Press, 2007), *The Foot of the Rainbow* (Red Dragonfly Press, 2010), *The Glory* (Red Dragonfly Press, 2015), *Windy Day at Kabekona: New and Selected Prose Poems* (White Pine Press, 2018), *Storm Island* (Red Dragonfly Press, 2020) and *Medicine Year* (Paris Morning Publications, 2022). He has also edited several books, most recently *Airmail: The Letters of Robert Bly and Tomas Tranströmer* (Graywolf Press, 2013). His prose work, *Poetry on the Side of Nature: Writing the Nature Poem as an Act of Survival*, is currently in preparation. He teaches poetry at the Loft Literary Center in Minneapolis and posts poems and essays on his web site at www.thomasrsmithpoet.com.

ABOUT THE ARTIST

John Ilg received a BFA and MFA from the University of Minnesota. His work has been in numerous solo and juried exhibitions nationwide; he has received many purchase prizes and jury awards.

Of this cover art, Ilg says: "The image was seen 'accidentally' at my wife's family farm near Willow River, MN. Looking east as the sun was setting in the late afternoon, I noticed the color all shaded down in the shadow valley in front of me and the brightly lit distant hillside, the moon coming up, a tiny house in the middle distance."

More of John's work can be seen at johnilg.com.

www.ingramcontent.com/pod-product-compliance
Lightning Source LLC
Chambersburg PA
CBHW060044030426
42334CB00019B/2479